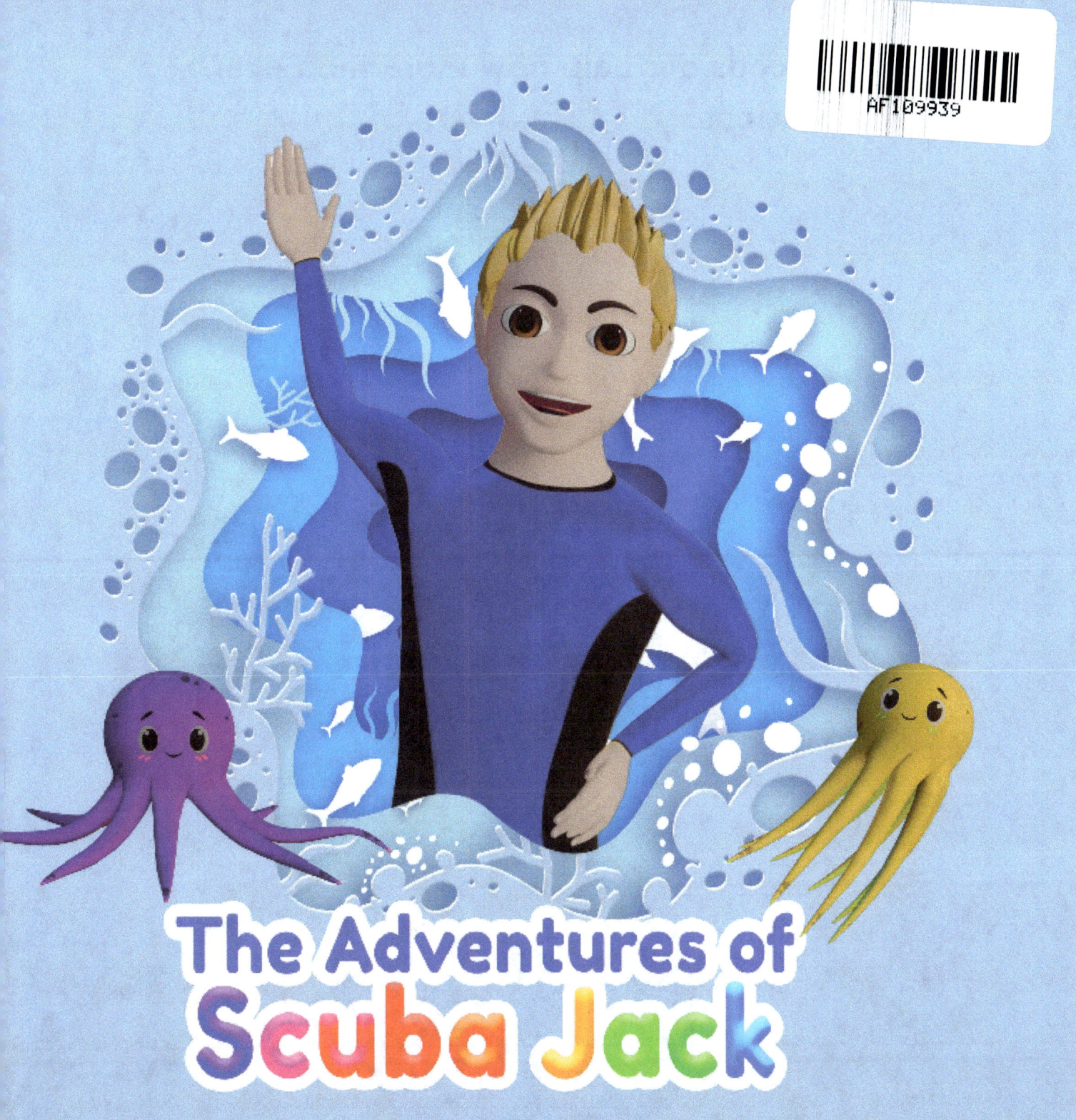

Visit us at
www.adventuresofscubajack.com
for more FUN Learning!

Our planet needs our help now more than ever.
Nature is precious.

Shine bright, little one, and watch the world ignite with your love and kindness.

Children may be little, but they can make a big difference in the world.

Shine bright, little one, and watch the world ignite with your love and kindness.

Bring **JOY** to those around you!
Be the reason someone smiles today.

Shine bright, little one, and watch the world ignite with your love and kindness.

Some children don't have anything to eat.
Offer them one of your snacks.

Shine bright, little one, and watch the world ignite with your love and kindness.

Shine bright, little one, and watch the world ignite with your love and kindness.

Every day is a chance to learn. Learn everything!

Shine bright, little one, and watch the world ignite with your love and kindness.

Some days may be hard for you! You may fail. Get up and adjust your crown and know you're special, designed by God.

Shine bright, little one, and watch the world ignite with your love and kindness.

Shine bright, little one, and watch the world ignite with your love and kindness.

The best way to predict your future is to create it.

Shine bright, little one, and watch the world ignite with your love and kindness.

Difficult roads often lead to beautiful destinations.

Shine bright, little one, and watch the world ignite with your love and kindness.

Focus on the step-in front of you and not the entire staircase.

Shine bright, little one, and watch the world ignite with your love and kindness.

There was a celestial dance in the heavens on the day you were born. That's how special you are!
You're the greatest gift of life. You may be little now, but you can make a big difference in this world.
You have special gifts, talents, and amazing ideas to share. You can do anything you set your mind to do!
Do great things, little one!

Shine bright! Don't ever let that light fade. Know that you are loved and that you matter always!

www.ingramcontent.com/pod-product-compliance
Lightning Source LLC
LaVergne TN
LVHW060134080526
838201LV00118B/3048